WORKING FROM HOME

How to Make Money from Home and Grow Your Income Fast, with No Prior Experience!

Start Making Money with the Right Home Business In 2021. (Guide for Beginners)

Jack Simon

TABLE OF CONTENT

INTRODUCTION

When the subject of creating passive income comes up, an Internet business is touted to be one of the most effective strategies with good reasons to back it up. Internet marketing is a very low-cost venture that almost everyone can start up, and it allows you to advertise to a worldwide market from your living room or bedroom. The truth is that you can make serious money free on the web! All you need to know is where to start. If you want to work from home, you have two options:

One: Make money online.

Two: Make money offline i.e. not using your computer.

This book will cover how to make money online as well as the gimmicks of making money offline. So, here's a question you can ask yourself, and then you'll be shown how to make money from your room's corner!

How much do you want to earn and how much time can you put into your home-based business?

And the right answers will help you figure out which method of working from home is best for you. If your response is something along the lines of "I want to make $2000 - $5000 per month in passive income and I have plenty of time to develop my company," I would advise you to either design websites (no prior experience required) or get busy with affiliate marketing. You can do this by selling other people's goods on the internet without having to purchase something or negotiate with customers. These are two of the most common online money-making options.

If your response is "I just want to make lots of money quickly and I don't have a lot of time," AdWords is best suggested option for you to make money. This is an online advertising program. You will need a budget for this and it is recommended that you set it very low while you are testing whether your ad campaign works. What products you can advertise. The most economic route is to become an affiliate (as recommended in the last paragraph) and sell other people's information products.

If your response is "I just want some extra part-time income without having to learn something new," I recommend taking online surveys. It's a straightforward and easy way to supplement your income. You know how people sometimes approach you in the street with their clipboards wanting to ask you questions for market research? This is an online version of that. Companies need people's opinions and will pay for them. They save money doing this online because they don't have to pay someone to ask you the questions!

If you like sharing your thoughts and opinions with the world and would like to get paid for doing so, I suggest you make money blogging. A blog is essentially an online journal that you can create for free. So, if you're on a tight budget, this could be a good place to start. You earn money from your blog by placing advertisements and links on it.

It's great to select a specialty to write about or advertise about with all of these money-making methods. Otherwise, there's too much competition and it could take you ages to actually make money. For instance, you will do better with a niche subject like bridal chokers rather than jewellery which is too broad a subject.

You also need to understand that keywords play a vital role in the success of any blogger or affiliate marketer. Wordtracker is a good tool to help you with keywords. I recommend you don't focus too much on the most popular keywords because, again, there's probably too much competition for them. Go for the more obscure ones and you are more likely to get good results! If you feel passionate about your business success will surely follow.

The current economy is certainly not an easy one to live in. Thousands of people are quitting their jobs, after all, and there does not seem to be enough money to go around. This is never a good thing! In fact, it makes it very difficult to survive in the world we currently inhabit. Despite the fact that the unemployment rate is rising, rates for products and services tend to be rising as well. In truth, none of this makes any sense at all. The good news is you can still make a buck if you know how to get started. You may be asking yourself, in today's world, how can I generate revenue? But the answer varies from person to person. There are opportunities you should consider.

The next time you ask yourself, how I can make money, think about your personal computer. After all, no one ever said you had to go out of your own residence in order to make more money! At least not in this modern age of technology and instant access to information should anyone claim ignorant. You are put in touch with the world and general society instantly these days when you have online access. Now, before you dismiss the World Wide Web, you should consider all that it really has to offer. There are business opportunities galore concerning the Internet. You simply have to be open-minded and have a good idea of what it is you want to do. You can make a lot of money by owning only a personal computer connected to the internet!

CHAPTER ONE
HOW TO AVOID THE WRONG ADVICE BEFORE YOU START TO WORK FROM HOME

The benefit that we all can enjoy in modern society is that we can work from home effectively and be there to raise our children. The internet and conference call can turn any home office into a growing and strong business environment.

There has been a large shift from office-based commuting to home-based commuting. Working from home eliminates the stress of traffic to the office; interoffice politics and missing a great deal of your home life. This has spawned a great deal of "work from home opportunities" that promise's the dream lifestyles but deliver's nightmares.

The price of wrong advice can be very costly and damage your reputation. It takes good judgment and patience to successfully work from home. There are a few essentials you need to prepare before working on your own; I call them the 5 c's of working from home.

1. Commitment

You need to be absolutely committed to making it work. There must not be any room for uncertainty.

2. Communicate with Family

Your family has to be informed that even though you will be working from home, you will have a schedule to follow and they must honour it without leaving tasks to be done that interfere with your work. Trust me! The groceries can be bought like before you stayed at home. Not during the weekday when you should be working.

3. Clear goals

You must write clearly what you wish to achieve in the long, medium and short term. A good place to start is determining how much money you want to earn per month (especially if you wish to start your business). Remember, this is work, not a hobby. You must make money by next month or risk going backwards. Then define your strengths, weaknesses and personal interests. You must research clearly how you can make money from your interests (they will keep you going in the rough months ahead). After achieving the income you planned for 3 to 6 consecutive months without fail then you can indulge. You must also plan how you will invest the increased income to receive passive income. "Never put your eggs in one basket". Investing in a rental property that pays you regularly or reinvesting in adding more passive income from your business also helps build security.

4. Consult your team

This reason alone is why many online businesses and start-ups fail. Who should be on your team? Not your relatives or close friends unless they are the best. I work with this motto, *"Cheap advice is worth... and free advice is worth even..."* You need a lawyer, accountant, banker and your spouse. Why spouse? Because spouses keep you consistent by being there despite the highs and lows. Your team will also remind you when you are emotionally investing in something that is not working and will easily pick up scams based on their own interpretation. That said you still have to make up your own mind after listening to their advice.

5. Commit to doing it.

You will learn better from trial and error than anybody can teach you in a seminar, e-book or course. Just make sure you test and compile data to see what works and what does not. You must pay attention to the results so that you do more of whatever works and less of what does not work.

The benefits of studying to earn money online from home

Process of making passive income from home can be a great way to start making extra money that you can use in a number of ways.

If this is your first time working on creating online income for yourself it will be much like learning how to walk, read, write or ride a bike. It can be very challenging and it will require that you have the self-discipline to focus on learning what you need to learn and then doing what needs to be done until you reach your goal.

One of the primary reasons some people struggle to figure out how to make passive income is that they either do not work hard enough or they do not stick with it long enough. Think about when you were first learning any new skill such as walking, talking or learning to read and write, these things took time, effort and persistence. The same is true for learning how to make money online from home.

Despite the fact that it will be difficult, it can be very rewarding and life-enhancing. Here are a few of the many different benefits that you can expect to enjoy:

- **Spending more time with your family and friends**

This will come about as a direct result of your ability to develop good time management skills. By effectively organizing your time and completing the tasks necessary to achieve your objectives, you will have more leisure time to spend as you please.

- **Increased Time Flexibility**

Because you will be your own boss, you should plan the workload so that you can complete tasks when it is convenient for you. In some cases, you may choose to work during the early morning hours, while everyone else is asleep or you may choose to work other non-traditional hours throughout the day.

- **Reduced Work Expenses**

You will be saving on a variety of different work-related costs such as travel expenses, meals and work clothes. In addition, you may qualify for certain small business tax deductions as well.

- **Improved efficiency**

Because you will be working alone, you can focus for long uninterrupted periods to complete your daily tasks; this can allow you to become much more productive throughout your day.

- **Unlimited Income Potential**

Unlike a traditional job if you choose to start your own online business then you will not be trading hours for dollars and you will be able to leverage the 24hour, 7 days a week availability of the internet to work for you continuously. This can be one of the smartest ways to start working on creating long term financial success for yourself by creating online passive income.

Making the best decisions when trying to make money online.

Make Money from Home if You Have the Right Attitude!

The Internet has opened up a world of possibilities for earning money without having to work in the conventional workforce. If you want to work from home and earn money, you can find a way to do it.

However, it's not an automatic process. To be successful, you'll need to have the right outlook toward the process. It's basically a three-step process. If you're serious about making a good living as a web-based entrepreneur, you'll want to be certain that you fully understand the importance of these three aspects of the right overall mindset.

First and foremost, you must embrace the fact that success will necessitate some effort. You'll see a few advertisers who'll be happy to tell you that you can become an overnight billionaire if you send them a nice chunk of your hard-earned cash, but the truth is that you will need to put in some effort and time to start building a serious income. Don't get excited about working two hours per day while your business acts as an automatic moneymaking machine, running in the background. In time, you will build passive revenue streams that will reduce your workload. However, you need to put in the time necessary to build the right foundation.

Second, you'll need to understand that the best way to go from novice to earner is to follow a proven underlying system. If you latch onto a good blueprint devised by someone who knows what it really takes to make money from home using the Internet, you'll be in a great position to experience success. On the contrary, those who approach online business as a "Do It Yourself" project often struggle and surrender before they start to see results. Invest in a smart, proven system and follow the recommendations. It's not necessary to come up with something new or make errors that could have been avoided.

Finally, you must learn to resist the temptations that come with having your own company. Even though you won't have a boss or an employer breathing down your neck, if you'd like to make extra money on the side, you'll need to stay focused and on-task. The freedom of being your own boss is wonderful, but too many people find it hard to stay on track when they're suddenly in control of their own time. Effective entrepreneurs are also distinguished from those who never really get anything done by their willingness to keep focused and act responsibly. Make the necessary adjustments to remain on schedule, and consider investing some time in learning about time management strategies--investment in learning can pay huge dividends.

If you can develop this three-pronged outlook, you can make money from home. Those who realize the importance of putting forth an effort, following a smart plan and resisting the temptations that come with the newfound freedoms of entrepreneurship are much more likely to reach their financial goals.

CHAPTER TWO
BRILLIANT PERSONAL FINANCE TIPS (THAT WILL HELP YOU BUILD WEALTH)

A financially free person is that person who can spend money on his satisfaction anytime he/she wishes to do so without much sweating. This necessitates a series of well-thought-out measures taken over time, as wealth does not accumulate overnight. According to one theory, if all the wealth in the world is evenly distributed among all people, the money will eventually return to its rightful owners in a short period of time.

The following are a few of the most effective tips to keep in mind if you want to increase your wealth.

Get Education

You become a master not just another tourist on the plane if you have a solid foundation of everything you do. The risk of a half- or no-education is that you will run out of ideas and be stalked at some stage during your journey into your new venture. Approach experts and gain authentic information from them. You can also read books because readers are leaders.

Go All Out To Solve Problems

Those who are controlling the world and will continue to do so are those who choose to solve problems because the world will continue to battle with one challenge or the other and the world will keep evolving from those challenges. As a result, those few who take the lead to address these issues will be crowned kings and queens. The desire to travel around the planet quicker and more efficiently gave rise to modern transportation devices, and the desire to save more human lives prompted scientists to develop various medicines to treat a variety of diseases. Identify the challenges people around you are facing and go all out to solve them before you know it, you will build a wealthy dynasty for yourself.

Don't Follow the Crowd

Many people want to do what the crowd is doing simply because they believe others are making money from it, without considering what it takes to be effective in those areas, whether they be emotional, physical, or spiritual. For example, these days, every young girl wants to work in the fashion and beauty industry, regardless of what that means. We have all neglected the fact that what made Mr A successful might totally ruin Mr B. Understand your being and strive to be unique at all times. Your wealth will keep rising.

Take Risks

Taking risks entails seizing and exploiting any and all opportunities that present themselves. A lot of people are too afraid to take risks. It's a good idea to *aim for the stars even if you miss, you'll at least have walked on the moon*. Life is a gamble in and of itself.

Develop A Savings And Investing Habit

Whatever your revenue is, learn to set aside a portion of it and spend it wisely. A lot of people spend their income and try to save what is left which is most likely going to remain nothing for savings. On the contrary, save first from your income before spending what is left. This is easy to do by not living beyond your regular earnings.

Work For Yourself (Be An Entrepreneur)

Check the list of the rich people in the world, entrepreneurs will always top the list because their income has no limit. When you work for someone or a company, your income will always be limited no matter how intelligent, dedicated and committed you may be. After all, you won't earn more than the business owner, your boss.

Have A Fearful Dream

They say the world is only for those who believe in the beauty of their dreams. Get a dream and make plans to achieve it at all times because you never know when you will have the opportunity to do so. Do not simply stop dreaming; work towards realizing those dreams by meticulously preparing and carrying out your plans.

Find Additional Sources of Income

Financial problems often stem from inadequate revenue as opposed to expenditure problems. If you are following a budget, watching your spending, and still have issues building your wealth, you should look into generating more than one source of income. More income sources tend to provide more financial stability and give you residual cash to save or invest.

Improve Your Job Skills

Although it might not seem directly related to your finances, job security is an important part of your financial identity, because it determines how regular your paycheck is. Make sure you own the necessary skills to remain effective in the future. It may involve getting extra certifications. And, it could mean returning to school to pursue a degree that will prepare you for a more secure job.

Set Specific Financial Goals

Use the numbers and dates to explain what you want to achieve with your money, not just words. How much debt will you pay off – and when? How much do you want to have saved, and by what date? You should do all that is humanly possible to follow your plans to achieve your goals.

Get Insured

Your finances will be covered if you purchase the appropriate insurance coverage. Popular forms of insurance include auto and renter insurance or home insurance, life insurance, and health insurance if the employer does not provide it. It safeguards you from disasters that could ravage your resources.

Take Full Advantage of Employee Compensation

Additional employee benefits, such as dental care, eye insurance, and flexible spending plans, are commonly available at some businesses. Any of these suggestions will help you create wealth by removing the need to pay for necessary expenses out of your own pocket. If you take the time to think about your options, you'll be able to get the most out of your employee benefits.

Reduce Your Regular Expenses

When building your wealth, you should consider cutting down some unnecessary expenses. While you might not be able to eliminate all fixed expenses, you may reduce variable expenses by being adaptable and frugal with your spending, especially on clothing and entertainment.

The typical culprits you can look at our electricity consumption, utility costs choose cheaper insurance plans and buy your food at a discount at bulk stores.

Give up Eating Out

Reduce your restaurant visits and you'll be surprised by how much money you'll save if you start cooking your meals at home. You can begin once a week and save the extra money in a safe place. Then start thinking about what you'll bring to work for lunch.

Pay off your debts first.

Begin by making a list of all of your existing debts, including credit card debt, student loan debt, and auto loan debt, and determine the smallest amount you owe to stay current on each debt. To get out of debt as quickly as possible, make a debt payment plan and stick to good spending habits. Maintain financial discipline to avoid adding to your debt excessively before your next paycheck arrives.

Track Your Net Worth

The variance between your revenue and total income is your net worth, and it's the big-picture figure that will tell you where you stand financially. Keep an eye on this number because it will help you keep track of your progress toward wealth development and building, as well as warn you if you're falling behind.

Get Money Buddies

When you put yourself amid financially disciplined and focused friends, their ways and habits tend to rub off on you such that you can also learn from them to build your own wealth and be financially free

Evaluate Purchases by Cost Per Use

Buying a fashionable shirt over a simple shirt can appear to be more cost-effective—but only if you overlook the quality factor. Consider how many times you'll use or wear the new tech toy, kitchen gadget, or fashion piece before deciding whether it's worth it. Simply put, don't overspend on trendy materials, which can be astronomically more costly than standard materials.

Do Everything Possible Not to Cash Out Your Retirement Account Early

Taking a portion of your pension funds too soon will have a variety of consequences for you. To begin with, you are undermining all of your hard work in saving the money. Also, you will be heavily penalized for early withdrawal by your pension funds managers. Most painful, you will get hit with another tax bill for the money you withdraw. Because of all of these reasons, cashing out early can only be seen as a last resort.

When You Get a Raise, Raise Your Retirement Savings also

Since your dream is to multiply your retirement savings by having more leftover cash, there is no way to do so. When you get a raise, the first thing you can do is increase your retirement contributions and immediately boost your savings. It's a fantastic way to increase your wealth.

The words of the founding fathers of the richest family in the world (Nathan Rothschild) is just true when you look at the settings across the world *"Give me all the money in a country and I care less about who makes the laws in that country".*

Your financial security is in your possession if and only if you are willing to take the risk.

What is passive income?

Passive income as opposing to active income is accrued gains made from 'inactive' involvement in a making money process. This technique supplements your full-time job as well as various financial investments one does and they are great because not only that you do not need your own product or service, but you do not even need to keep promoting them every single month just to keep the money coming.

However, don't be fooled by scammers who provide offers that promise every lazy marketer a dream. Here are the main benefits of joining programs that bring huge passive income. You do not need to spend time researching and developing your own products or services. You can get started right away with minimum guidance. You get paid for every sale you make and recurring income thereafter.

If you're up and running, you'll have more time to pursue other avenues of income conveniently. You can also enter partner programs with a variety of items on the internet.

There are several services that are pyramid schemes, as well as numerous scams. To be pragmatic, even the simplest lazy form of online passive income campaign involves some form of work and effort put in. Don't be boned by scam artists that offer campaigns that work for the laziest of the lazy. In reality, it just does not work that way. What they don't tell you is you need to pay a hefty sum for that.

Here is the real fact - earnings from a passive income do not require the direct involvement of the owner or merchant in the business. For instance, if you are publishing a book online, all you need to spend is some fees for posting your product and the agreed percentage cut that was given to the vendor for helping you to market the product. To get more exposure, you will need to spend some on third-party marketing agencies online such as link building services, banner ads, blogging and reviews.

Passive income can be semi-automated and fully automated. Semi-automated are methods that require you to build some groundwork before your campaign can operate and start generating income streams. This method needs a strong foundation and full commitment at the very early stage. The failure to secure this will result in failure.

Semi-automated methods require very small startup costs and sometimes, almost free. Some examples of this are niche blogging, banner and link ads, affiliate reviews, online real estate broker, e-commerce affiliates or personal e-commerce store etc. Fully automated methods are referred to as the lazy marketer's method. This system is perfected by their vendors so that when you register and pay, they will tap your details into it and start making money. The advantages are you don't have to worry about the groundwork such as the setup, installation and marketing. This is because those tasks come in the form of what you have already paid for.

Some examples of this are turnkey websites for banner and link ads, affiliate mini-sites, automated email lists, turnkey e-commerce sites, money-making software like forex, membership sites, training/coaching, investments etc.

Creating a passive income may not make you money, despite the fact that the end aim is to make big money in a passive manner. When creating a passive income, you are creating a system that does not trade time for money and in the process of creating this system, you may spend more than you earn.

Many people can't get past the idea of losing money before making money. That's why most people fail to create their first passive income online. On the contrary, those who are 'lucky enough to create their first stream of passive income online will continue to create the second stream and third stream because they're used to the idea of losing some money before getting it all back, multiplied. Another reason is that with their first passive income established, their risk appetite is higher and they are more willing to lose. The last reason is that they are more experienced now. If you've just started out, go find a job to make money. But don't spend too much time on it. Take 3-5% of your monthly income and most of your spare time to create a passive income online. What you need to note that even passive income can be made from home; you must not forget the responsibilities of being a citizen. Passive income is taxable, applies to all fully automated businesses, especially web-based.

Essential Tips For Creating Passive Income

There is something grand when you decide to give up on the 9 to 5 world. Joining the many people that are carving out a living without spending hours and hours on end in jobs that they hate abound through every single industry. If you are ready to take on a different route to making a living, you are going to want to look into the world of creating passive income through staying home. Working from home, and online is a great way to launch your new life. Imagine not having to put in 8 hours a day to make more money in less time. This is a real option and it comes with knowing and applying a few tips moving forward. The specific steps needed to start something will vary based on your choice of options. Some of the different options include freelance work, content writing, being an online business owner, affiliate marketing, etc. However, here are the basic steps that you can take to make sure that you make the right choice and have the best chances of making so much cash without stepping out of your home.

- **Spend Time Learning Your Business**

The first thing that you are going to want to do is simple, spend time learning the business. If you do not learn the business that you have in front of you, you're not going to make money. Many people try to rush the process, especially when it comes to joining an MLM (Multi Level Marketing) scenario. Do not rush anything. The more you rush through the learning process, the more likely you are to lose money in the long term. You'll want to find a way to figure out how to apply what you're learning to real-world situations on the web, and that takes time. Also, one of the most important things that you can do is to make sure that you find something that will be profitable for you both in the short term and long term. Finding an evergreen market, where people are always spending money or a rising trend can help set you up for long term business success.

- **Invest In Your Equipment**

One of the biggest hurdles that people have when trying to work with passive income is their equipment fails. Find a way to purchase a new laptop or tablet that is solely for your business needs. You want to be connected anywhere, and everywhere. You also want to have the security of knowing that you are going to be able to make gains when you need to. Investing in your equipment will pay off down the line, that's for sure. Do not skimp on this. It's easy to miss the mark here. Don't allow yourself to lose sight of the importance of having the right equipment for your quest to make money on the web.

- **Document The Process**

If you are going to make a go at creating passive income online, make sure that you document the process. Start a blog and talk about the difficulties, and successes that you have. This is a very important step in the process. The reason why is simple. People are looking for this information. They are looking to see real-life stories about people that are trying to make money online. If you post this information and you work within the right parameters, you will end up with a huge leap forward. Document everything, and watch your income soar.

- **Monetize Your Pages Early**

At the early stages of your business, make sure that you are monetizing your pages. Even if you don't have a large audience built yet. You want to make sure that you have elements that can make you a good income in place. If you do not focus on this, you are going to end up losing focus fast. Monetization shouldn't be relegated to when you have an audience in place, because you're going to lose them if you start throwing ads around your page. Start early and keep them in place.

• Do Not Expect Millions Up Front

Of all the tips that you can work through, this is one of the most important. Do not think that you are going to be a millionaire from working online or at any gig fast. Sure, some have made it happen fast, but chances are you will not. If you are realistic about what you're doing, and you just keep working at it, you could make six figures. However, don't believe the notion of making millions within a week or overnight. There are a lot of marketers that will sell you on this dream, and it's a false hope. Don't get caught up in that.

- **Do Not Throw In The Towel Too Early**

The biggest thing that you are going to want to keep in mind, especially if you've never really worked in this arena, is to not give up. Giving up too early can end up causing you a lot of regrets. There are plenty of marketers that tried to create passive incomes but failed. They gave up too soon. Sometimes you have to work a great deal to reach the summit of passive options. Take your time, learn the ropes, and just keep going step by step. Sometimes it takes a little longer, but it will come through if you're disciplined.

- **Find A Mentor**

Once you have identified the type or area of online business that you would like to focus on, the next most important thing to do is to find a mentor or get the training that you need to become successful in that area. This goes hand in hand with learning any new skill or ability. You will always do better if you have someone to help you or show you how things should be done.

- **Implement A System**

The next and final step is to develop a system for creating consistent results. This will involve a lot of testing and improving and this will be an ongoing part of generating income from home so you must be able to create and implement a system that works in producing profitable results. If you work at it long enough and hard enough (put your best effort into it) then you will reach the point where you will be able to make money from home online and reap all of the many different benefits that go along with this accomplishment.

CHAPTER THREE
COMPLETING SURVEYS AND FREELANCE WRITING

Completing Surveys

Creative people can always find ways to make money at home. Several alternative forms of earning money without leaving the comfort and convenience of your own home have emerged as a result of the internet. The most significant consideration when choosing a profession is that it meets your financial needs, your attitude, and your desire to participate. Pay-Per-Click possibilities provide certain people with a source of passive income. Others prefer the more hands-on approach to freelance writing or data entry jobs. Of course, you can also choose to complete surveys for pay and return them to the companies that need the information. This is an area lots of companies require experts to help them carry out researches and give reports. These reports are needed to make useful decisions such as the customers' acceptance of a new product to be introduced into the market, contemplation on expansion. You get all the info you need on the internet without leaving your home.

You make money at home by completing surveys for companies who want to find out how consumers feel about their product or service. Surveys are often used to conduct research for theses, dissertations, and other forms of research papers, usually for graduate work. In either type of survey completing work, you just need to work through the list of questions about your own experiences with a particular product, service or subject. Once the survey is completed, you submit it to the company or organization that requested the information and later you receive payment for the time you spent.

Freelance Writing

Completing writing projects for others is a wide-open field for you to make money at home using the internet. Freelance sites provide information about various projects that buyers are trying to complete by contracting with service providers. Writing insightful and interesting articles on almost every topic found on the internet is a common part of the job. Buyers often choose content pages with unique keywords included to put on their websites instead of posts. The keywords help to bring visitors to the website through search engine links. The process of providing keyword-rich articles and content for websites is known as search engine optimization. One method for making money at home is to write freelance articles online for other people. You can do this from the comfort of your own home and make a few bucks for each article that you produce. Now, this might not sound like a great deal, but just think how it would add up if you wrote about 15 articles each day, and did this every single day of the month. You would be bringing in well over a thousand per month in income, just from writing freelance articles. Now the people who are ordering these articles are not stupid.

They are investing in the writing and they are publishing the content online. You can, if you choose, make money on the other side of this fence as well. Instead of being paid to write articles for other people, you could simply write articles for yourself and publish them on your own websites. You can even publish articles on a totally free website that you set up yourself and you can still make good money from it. This is a bit more of a long term strategy than freelancing but you can build up a nice stream of passive income this way.

What to Do As a Beginner Freelance Writer

If like many other people, you have thought about the possibility of making money from being a freelance writer, you are probably fired up with enthusiasm, but unsure of how to begin. Freelance writers work in a variety of fields, including ghostwriting books, writing essays, blog posts, editing for magazines, writing newspaper columns, and just about every other type of writing you might think of. With such a vast array of areas in which to operate, how do you go about choosing your niche and getting started? Below is my advice on this.

If you are considering dipping your toe into the freelance pool, then hopefully you have experience of writing for publication. If you haven't, don't worry too much about it as there are ways of achieving this that may not be as difficult as you imagine. The purpose of getting your name into print is twofold. Firstly, the boost to your confidence will be immeasurable. Secondly, whatever you can show to a potential client regarding your previous work will help you to win jobs early in your career. So how do you go about getting published? Well, there are ways to do this without landing a major book deal or being a journalist. There are a massive number of places online where the written word is sort after by webmasters. Content has to come from somewhere. Start by writing what interests you, whether it is short stories or informative articles - whatever it is will be useful. Think about writing letters to the editor of your local newspaper, or short filler for a magazine. It is writing practice and it gets your name out there. So what next? Writing is hard work. If you don't enjoy what you do, then it is even harder. By trying several different types of writing, you not only improve, but you get to find out where your interest really lies. Armed with this knowledge, I would suggest you try one of the many freelance marketplaces online where you can bid for work. You will need to build up your writer's profile which will include your previous work and specialist areas. Remember to act professionally on these sites, as getting a bad reputation will come back to bite you when it comes to winning work.

You Don't Have To Be a Professional

A lot of people think that they couldn't possibly become a freelance writer because they have not been to university to study journalism. This could not be further from the truth, in fact, the majority of freelance writers cashing in have never studied any form of writing at a university level. In fact, many writers do not even speak English as their first language who are cashing in $30-$50/hour. All you need is a good command of the English language to work as a freelance writer. It is preferable, but not mandatory, to be a native English speaker.

CHAPTER FOUR
DATA ENTRY AND PAY-PER-CLICK

DATA ENTRY

You can make money at home easily by completing various types of data entry projects. These may be routine secretarial or clerical jobs. They may be jobs that include the creation or maintenance of a database. Data entry jobs can include transcription of materials from audio or video files. Because there is so much variety in the type of work that qualifies as data entry jobs, most people can find an opportunity that fits perfectly with their personality, experience and financial needs. Data entry jobs take minimal investment to get started and have the additional advantage of you being able to set your own working hours.

The internet is filled with a plethora of different opportunities and ways to make money online. Data entry is one of the fast-growing ways of making a lot of money from your home. While this is a legitimate chance for an entrepreneur to profit big, you should understand the nitty-gritty of the field well.

Transcribing data into another format, usually using a computer program, is what data entry entails. There are several different types of data and records that need to be entered and transcribed, which opens up a lot of doors for online businesses. Some of the types of data you may work with include handwritten documents, data from spreadsheets, and simple information like names and addresses.

There is no doubt that companies do not always have the time to collect and professionally present documents. To take advantage of a data entry job, you need to be a proficient typist and be capable of inputting codes into programs and files. Ultimately, you need to be able to read off longhand or typewritten documents accurately.

The simplest mistakes can bankrupt a business, which is why they outsource work to professionals. A single incorrect letter, number, or symbol may cause a program's entire security function to fail. If something is entered wrongly in a spreadsheet, for instance, this can result in the information or message being delivered inaccurately.

This type of job does require a great deal of focus and concentration. While it can be exhausting and challenging, there are different degrees of difficulty depending on how serious you want to take it.

One of the many benefits of having a data entry job is the ability to work wherever you want. You do not necessarily have to work in an office or workplace. You can work at your home sitting on the living room couch if you prefer to. This gives you a tremendous amount of freedom and flexibility to work when you want wherever you want.

As you begin looking for offers and job opportunities within this field, be cautious of taking up a scam offer. You can identify these as anything that promises you to work as long as you pay a fee. There are several scams all over the internet you need to be wary of. This is why you must take the time to look at each opportunity closely to determine whether or not it is a legitimate offer.

A data entry work online could be just what you've been looking for. It's straightforward, gives you a great deal of flexibility, and it's fun to work around. This is unquestionably a worthwhile online opportunity.

PAY PER CLICK (PPC)

Pay per click programs allow you to make passive income from advertising. It is also an easy way to make money at home. This type of home-based business opportunity requires only a very small investment to get started and the potential for increased revenue streams is almost unlimited. Once the ads are set up, you don't need to spend a lot of time on the pay-per-click program, and the money just keeps rolling in.

Pay per click (PPC) is an online advertisement model in which consumers see your advertisements as they search for topics relevant to the product or service you're selling. Only when your ad is clicked on can you (the advertiser) pay the host. Your ads are displayed only when a search engine user types in a search request using your chosen keywords. To ensure you are successful with your pay per click efforts, the following are tips to guide you.

1. Get Organized

As an example, consider a surgeon who wants to promote her bariatric surgery program. She knows that prospective patients use a variety of terms to refer to the type of surgeries she performs: "gastric bypass," "lap band," "weight loss surgery," etc. Creating a plan that combines these search words with the same ad, on the other hand, is likely to fail. What is the reason for this? Since effective PPC advertisement requires pinpointing a user's search words. As a result, if a potential future patient types in "bariatric surgery" and sees an ad with the term "Gastric Bypass," the consumer is more likely to miss the ad and look for one with the words "bariatric surgery" in the description.

To address this issue, advertisers need to create multiple ad groups. For instance, it makes sense to have a bariatric surgery ad group, a weight loss surgery ad group, a lap band ad group, a gastric bypass ad group, and so on. And for each ad group, the advertiser will need an appropriate set of keywords to trigger the ads to serve. Yes, this kind of specificity is labour-intensive. Yes, it requires a great deal of time, effort, and thought. However, this kind of specificity is an essential ingredient in developing an effective PPC advertising program, and it's the kind of advice that a knowledgeable provider will prescribe as part of its pay per click services.

2. Take Advantage of Banner Advertising

While most of us think of pay per click advertising like Google AdWords, the paid search includes a wide range of advertising options, including banner ads. These are diagrams crafted ads that appear at the top of websites or inside the content of others. They frequently involve illustration, and animation.

Many people assume these ads are sold by the owners or proprietors of the websites on which they appear. Sometimes, that is the case. However, more often than not, these ads appear in space that is "rented" by Google and other pay per click advertising placement companies. In these instances, the ads served to users based on the keywords the advertiser has identified as relevant to their product or service. Going back to the bariatric surgery scenario, a gastric bypass surgery advertisement may be shown to users who are visiting a website devoted to diet, fitness, and weight loss.

Typically, banner ads generate far fewer clicks than their text counterparts. However, that's not necessarily a bad thing because banner ads can reach many more internet users without incurring any cost. Remember, pay per click advertisers only pay when an internet user clicks on their ads. As a result, if an ad is served to thousands of people but no one clicks on it, the advertiser receives no compensation. Thousands of potential buyers are already exposed to the advertisement. In this regard, banner advertising can be an effective way to build brand awareness at a very affordable price.

3. Monitor, Modify and Maintain Your Campaign

A pay per click advertising program that is effective today can easily become ineffective tomorrow. That's because the competitive environment is constantly changing. New advertisers enter the arena. Existing advertisers change their bids. And website content changes which can influence the relevance and quality scores of ads. Prepare to closely track, constantly change, and faithfully manage your

PPC campaign if you want to introduce a successful PPC program. Keep an eye out for the ads that get the most views and have the highest number of clicks. Determine which keywords are the most profitable, and be prepared to raise the bid for these terms if appropriate.

Also, attach importance to keywords that are producing clicks on your ads but aren't important. In these cases, you can define "bad keywords" that will prevent your advertising from being shown. As a consequence, you won't have to pay for clicks from people who aren't likely to buy your goods or services. In the end, a pay per click advertisement campaign is a complex entity that necessitates continuous monitoring. As a result, many businesses hire a specialist pay-per-click advertisement firm. Of course, if you use a PPC service provider, make sure the organization subscribes to your campaign and tracks, modifies, and manages it as required.

CHAPTER FIVE
AFFILIATE MARKETING

Whether you want to earn a bit of extra cash in your spare time or become a kitchen table millionaire in the next 3 years, there is one method of making money from home that has stood the test of time. And that method is affiliate marketing!

If you have never heard of affiliate marketing before then you may be wondering what it is. Well, quite simply it involves promoting other people's products for a commission. These items are frequently informational, such as the ebooks available on the ClickBank marketplace.

There are many benefits to endorsing other people's goods. It means you don't have to spend countless hours creating your own product, so you can start seeing money in your bank account hours from now, instead of months down the line. There are also no customer care problems to deal with, so you won't be glued to your phone all day answering emails.

This is fantastic news because you will be able to maintain your current lifestyle while still meeting all of your responsibilities. Maybe you don't want to quit your job until you are making enough money? Or perhaps you need to look after your kids during the day? If so, then affiliate marketing is the answer you are looking for!

Some of the exciting benefits of affiliate marketing:

- **Less stress**

One of the reasons you are probably researching ways on how to make money online is because you want less stress in your life. Well, affiliate marketing can definitely offer you that. Just imagine working from the comfort of your own home every day with no boss looking over your shoulder every few minutes. Wouldn't you feel a lot more relaxed throughout the day? You sure would!

- **Flexibility**

Many people who make money from home do so because they want the flexibility that being self-employed brings. Maybe you only want to work 3 hours a day? Or perhaps you can only work for 4 days a week? As long as you are committed and focused, then you can certainly run an affiliate marketing business around your lifestyle.

- **Make a lot of money**

Do you want to learn how to make serious money from the comfort of your own home? It's really that easy. Promote goods that a large number of customers want, that pay out a 100% commission, and that have an established track record of delivering well. If you do this, then there is no reason at all why you can't make more money from home than you have ever made before in your life.

- **Passive income**

Most people who are interested in how to make money from a home dream about passive income. Let's face it: no one likes slaving away for hours on end every day, exchanging time for money, and constantly checking the clock.

You will start seeing daily passive income in your bank account by being an affiliate marketer. How cool will it be to set up a program and then just sit back and watch the tests roll in without having to do something else once the initial work is done?

How to Make Money as an Affiliate Marketer from Home

If you want to figure out how to make money on the internet as an affiliate marketer, there are a few steps you must take. Listed below are a few of them:

- **Pick a niche**

There are thousands of affiliate marketing programs out there in a wide variety of different marketers. When you first get started you will need to pick a niche before deciding what products you are going to promote. It is a good idea to pick a niche in one of the main markets - health, wealth and relationships - as this is where the majority of people have their main problems.

- **Start a blog**

One way to start getting traffic is to set up your own blog once you have chosen a niche. You can then start writing blog posts around your chosen subjects so that search engines such as Google can begin sending you traffic. This shall be further discussed in details in the next part of the book as you read on.

- **Build an email list**

One of the most overlooked steps for people making money online from home is that of building an email list. If your blog begins to receive traffic, you can set up an opt-in form or squeeze page so that people can access your mailing list. This means you will begin to develop a partnership with your subscribers and continue to promote affiliate deals to them. Sign up for an autoresponder service like Aweber to start to grow your email list.

How to make money from home... the really easy way

Listen! If you follow the steps above then you will start making money from home. The only problem is that it can take a lot of time and energy to get everything started.

A solution to this is to sign up with a company that does everything for you. Check out some of the top internet markers blogs. You will find they are usually involved with such companies. If they are involved that is a sign that there can be some good money to be made there.

Build Your Own Website Yourself

Working from home has never been more easily accessible than it is now. Multitudes of common people of all walks of life are using the internet to make a full-time or part-time living from home. If provided the proper instructions and the ability to do so, everyone can start making income from their personal laptop.

To use the social media, there are a variety of ways to earn money from home. I started out several years ago simply listing items on eBay and currently have several websites which now generate revenue 24 hours a day 7 days a week. When you start searching online for details on how to work from home, you will be flooded with many 'possibilities.'

Depending on how you would like to work you can choose from doing opinion surveys, selling items for profit on eBay or from your own website, listing other peoples products as an affiliate or even creating simple websites which generate income from placing other peoples adverts on the site. This may seem impossible for those with little in the way of internet experience, but now more than ever, and using the right programs anyone can build a website quite simply just by clicking a few buttons on a user-friendly interface. Everyone now can have a free interface to put something on the internet thanks to websites like Blogger.com and Hubpages.com. These sites allow you to create content and place it live on the internet allowing you to make money from adverts placed around your information.

You make money by people clicking on your adverts who have come to visit your site. Adverts are placed automatically which relate to the content on your site. This means that your visitors are more likely to be interested in clicking your adverts. The content of your site and the number of visits you generate will determine your income from these clicks. There are ways to determine your income potential before creating your content to maximize revenue from your websites. You can also place affiliate products on your site and earn income from generating sales. These products can be related to your content so your visitors are more likely to have an interest in them. Because these products are either in e-book style or website format, they are bought and sold automatically through the internet without you having to post anything or speak to anyone. It is all handled automatically once the system is set up. The beauty of this system is that it becomes a passive income, generating money on complete autopilot.

On-Demand Webcasting Can Be A Money-Spinner

The question many people ask is: "How do I benefit from Webinars and Webcasting?" you might wonder. "There's more than one way to skin a cat," as my uncle Leo from

Texas used to say. Your company, product, and service, as well as how you deliver them to your customers, will determine how you use Webinars to "bring home the bacon."

Many of my clients pack up their content to be delivered 'on-demand - creating modules of content to be spaced over time. This is known as an On-Demand Webcast vs. a live Webinar. You definitely turn templates and post them on your webpage, thus providing a library of content to which your customers can pay for "on-demand" or format access.

PowerPoint, video, monitoring, polling, analysis, analytics, and more will all be included in your documented sessions. It's a popular way to offer certification and professional development credits, as well as instruction, coaching, and other services.

You've created a passive income stream that removes the majority of the manual labor and helps you to reach many more people. You build it once and then repurpose it through a variety of platforms, including on-demand

Webcasts, offline CDs and DVDs, and home study courses, among others.

On-Demand Webcasts aren't the same as just filming a live Webinar and putting it up on your website and charging people to watch it. This is a viable choice for getting started with earning money. On-demand Webcasts are usually shorter in length, similar to an edited version of your Webinar, with a tighter emphasis on the content and the ability to provide more rich media than a live Webinar.

The key difference being - if you want to get paid to create content, you have to deliver the value and do it in a way that keeps people engaged and wanting more from you. There are several companies offering technology for you to create On-Demand Webcasts.

1) WebEx Presentation Studio

2) Brainshark Presentations

3.) AudioVideoWeb

Examine their hosting services, sign up for a free trial, and test each service to determine which package best meets your needs at a fair price. Remember that setting a fair price for On-Demand Webcasts requires balancing what you can charge for access to your On-Demand content against the expense of your chosen distribution network.

Finally, keep in mind that with periodic updates, your On-Demand library of training and coaching content will provide you with ongoing passive revenue. Since the manual labor of making your eLearning modules is done only once, you can now meet hundreds or thousands of people. You make money off it in the same way as a TV star does, musician or performing artist who is compensated for every time their 'content' is viewed or heard.

CHAPTER SIX
MAKING THE BEST FROM BLOG CREATION

Anyone can set up a blog and start writing content, but only a few of those blogs ever develop into money-making enterprises that generate a significant income stream. A lot of people who want to get into blogging end up getting confused about what exactly they should write about. It really isn't that hard. Passive income with blogging is more about frequency than specific content, though both are important. If you're blogging to earn money and you don't enjoy writing to begin with, you're wasting your energy. Blogging isn't a science, nor is it a predictable art form. You'll quickly get frustrated and angry if you don't have a strong passion for your art. Here are a few tips to help you on your journey to building a successful money-making blog right from the corner of your room.

1. Pick a Niche/Topic

Be specific on what you will write about. Define a topic or niche for yourself and design all your content around your chosen niche. This will assist you in not only focusing your writing, but also in developing digital products and services to augment your content. This enables you to attract customers, persuade customers with highly insightful posts, and then lure them with lead magnet blogs before turning them into existing clients. Look inwardly before choosing a niche or topic to start writing on so as not to run out of ideas and what to write on. You should pick a topic you are never tired of speaking on. Another way of getting a constant flow of quality content is looking at solving any of the challenges people are facing in your local environment and go ahead to find a solution to them. This attracts more audience and to your blog and once they become loyal to your blog, they can easily turn to your buyers because whatever you recommend to them as solutions to their challenges will be followed strictly.

2. Create useful content on a regular basis

You must build useful anchor content if you are serious about making your blog a success. It must be interesting, keyword-focused, educational, imaginative, and well-written. Don't write your blog solely for the benefit of search engines. Instead, write the content with a strong emphasis on humans while keeping the search engines and their needs in mind. Needless to say, it's an ability that can be learned by practice over time. It's also crucial that you make posts on a weekly and consistent basis. This will keep your audience yearning for more regularly. Consistency is key to winning over your audience; they mustn't be left hanging and waiting to hear from you because you will lose them as fast you were able to win them over. It is advisable to start from a monthly update at first and proceed to twice a month and then weekly. It is your choice.

3. Publishing regularly

To be a successful blogger, you need discipline, determination, drive, and focus. You must develop a publishing schedule and stick to it. Treat your blog like a traditional magazine. That usually has a publishing date each week or month and they stick to it because their readers expect them to. If you want to be a successful blogger, you ought to be publishing new quality content daily. If you can't do that, then decide on a publishing frequency that you can achieve and stick to it judiciously.

4. Select a Platform

Even though WordPress has been the most common website template, you can also use Tumblr, Blogger.com, and other similar platforms. Serious bloggers usually use a self-hosted Hosting service with their own domain. WordPress has a proven structure that is search engine friendly, very easy to set up and install and offers a large variety of free and paid design and functionality options.

5. Choosing a URL

You must also purchase a URL (Domain Name) for your blog after deciding on your favorite blogging site. There are a variety of resources available, with Namesco being one of the most well-known. Your URL should ideally be a '.com', since it is the strongest URL suffix on the internet, giving your blog an immediate advantage over other suffixed blogs. Your blog's URL need to be as simple as possible, keyword-rich, and contain only one wording combination if possible.

6. Promoting and Marketing your Content

Each blog post that you write needs to have links from other blogs and websites pointing to it. This will drive direct traffic from those sites, but also will build a network of links that will push your blog higher up the search engine rankings. You can either create links by guest posting on other relevant blogs and then hoping that someone can connect to your blog posts for you, or you can be proactive and link to your blog posts personally. Guest blogging, blog carnivals, groups, essay archives, blog comments, social media, and bookmarking are all useful resources to have on hand.

7. Sell Private Ads

Private advertising can come in a banner, click, or connection type. Also, you can make money writing supported posts where you write about, or review a product or service. The ways you use this to make money will differ. You could charge a one-time fee for a connection within a post, for example. If you are hosting banner ads, you might charge monthly. You can also contact advertisers yourself without any middleman.

8. Monetizing your Content

Once you have built an audience, you can start to think about making some money from your blog. Monetizing your content is simply the process of adding related links to products and services that you earn a commission on. You might even have your own goods or services that you want to promote if not, you can use your blog to sell other people's products just by adding a banner or link to your site content.

9. Install Google Analytic tools

These are tools needed to help you keep track of your efforts while building out your blog. This is a key to maintaining pace with innovation when you're using the URL promotion builder to drop links on social media and other locations so you can figure out where your traffic is coming from.

10. Be More Conversant With The Social Media

Building a blog isn't an easy feat to achieve. To help you along the road towards having a successful blog, you have to get social. Not only by connecting with other bloggers who share your interests, but also by sharing and communicating with others on social networking sites such as Facebook, Instagram, and other platforms, and share information.

It is noteworthy to state that all these steps are not one-size-fits-all. Individuals may need to tweak and combine them to really suit their condition and situation. Go with the ones that work best for you and simply drop the ones that seem not to work for you. Making money blogging can take a lot of patience but if you start from scratch, it can pay off in the long run. Just note that you don't have to use all those avenues at once to make money. Consider what other people are doing in your industry, and continue from there.

CHAPTER SEVEN
CRYPTOCURRENCY

What Is Cryptocurrency?

Cryptocurrencies are essentially a digital medium of exchange, living in a land of numbers and addresses. Unlike our centralized banking system, Cryptocurrencies are decentralized, transparent and allow users to exchange money without the need for a third party (for instance, a bank). For example, all Bitcoin transactions are registered and made public in a public ledger, which helps to ensure their validity and prevent fraud. To allow encrypted and anonymous transactions, these digital tools of exchange use cryptography and blockchain technology. In short, Bitcoin and other Cryptocurrencies allow for uncensored value transfer. The reason is due to its decentralized nature. It uses a consensus mechanism, known as the Nakamoto consensus, which establishes trust between untrusted parties. In simple words, it's a bearer asset that can be transferred digitally between two consenting parties with no reference of trust and without the right to be censored by a third party.

What Is A Blockchain?

Blockchain is the technology and protocols developed to store the information for Cryptocurrencies. Blockchain is essentially a digitized, decentralized public ledger that works like a cash book with credits and debits, and allows people to make transactions and store information. "At its core, blockchain is simply a database of sequential transactions on top of which one can define rules.

Information about each transaction within the Bitcoin network, for example, can be found in the Bitcoin blockchain. What is a page in a cash book is a block in the blockchain. If the block is "written", a new block is attached to write in. It creates a chain of blocks, thus the blockchain. The blockchain is visible to everyone, so there is perfect transparency. Each block has a #tag, which is a type of code, and this links each block to one another.

"The blockchain is a distributed database. It's not located on a central server that is accessed by all participants. Alternatively, each network participant keeps a copy of the blockchain on his machine, which is continuously synchronized with the network by downloading transaction blocks. Beyond Cryptocurrency, blockchain technology is now being investigated and used in a variety of fields, including insurance and banking.

What Is Mining?

Updates of trades must be spread around the system to keep the database up to date, which is where so-called "mining" fits in. This process is carried out not by individuals or businesses, but by thousands of machines linked to the Internet all over the world. These machines are referred to as "miners," but they should be referred to as "transaction-processing computers." Furthermore, to perform this processing safely, these machines must perform extremely complex calculations, essentially cracking the code and producing a #tag, which requires a significant amount of computational power, as well as costly and specialized processing equipment.

Someone – The machine owner must pay for this whole devices and power, so they must be paid for the money and effort they invested in making this system operational. For developing a #tag, they are compensated with newly mined Bitcoin. To summarize, all-new Bitcoin acts as a reward and incentive scheme for people to contribute their computers to the system to assist in transaction processing.

Brief History Of The Cryptocurrency

Since the introduction of Bitcoin (the world's first Cryptocurrency) by the mysterious Satoshi Nakamoto in 2009, Many other Cryptocurrencies have come into being, fuelling the frenzy. As a result, on 31st December 2017, the number of Cryptocurrencies available stood at 1381, including currencies like Ripple, Ethereum, Uhm, BigBoobsCoin and CryptoKitties!

In January 2017, Bitcoin, which has a net worth of more than $284 billion, began at $1000 per unit and had risen to about $20000 by mid-December 2017. Barely a week into 2018, the total Cryptocurrency market capitalization achieved a new all-time high (on 4th January), briefly rising above $770-billion amid a widespread altcoin rally. In line with international trends, demand in South Africa for Bitcoin has steadily increased. According to financial experts' report from intensive studies of the

Cryptocurrencies and trends for the past few years, explained the growth: "In 2015, a mere 300 Bitcoins traded per day in South Africa, at around R3 000 per coin; In December 2017 alone, Up to 2 000 Bitcoins are exchanged every day, with prices ranging from R200 000 to R250 000 per coin." However by the 6th of February 2018, Bitcoin had dropped to R76 500, demonstrating the uncertainty of Cryptocurrencies and the risks that come with it. As we speak, the total liquidation of the world's Cryptocurrency stands at about 2trillion dollars in total. That's a staggering amount of free money as they call it in the Cryptocurrency world.

How to Buy Cryptocurrency?

As much as the profit margin on investment in Cryptocurrency is very high and lucrative, it should be noteworthy that Cryptocurrencies are extremely volatile and you could lose a lot of money if you are not aware of the risks. However, should you decide to go ahead, the steps below are the detailed processes to guide you.

The first step to buying a cryptocurrency like Bitcoin is registering on any great international website of your choices such as www.luno.com, www.binance.com and other currently large and legitimate Cryptocurrency exchange companies. These companies operate in the world to facilitate Bitcoin to any currency trades between registered users. Other Cryptocurrency exchange companies you can also register on are www.coindirect.com/za or www. altcoin trader.co.za.

Once you've registered, verify your identity and your account has been validated, you deposit money via your bank into the account created and receive a reference number. You are now ready to buy a Bitcoin or part of any coin of your choice. You can either buy at the current price, at a lower price through a matching transaction (where a seller asks a slightly lower price than the going rate, which matches what the buyer is prepared to pay) or even just a small stake, say, $50 of a Bitcoin. A transaction fee is also charged by many of these sites.

The Effect of Cryptocurrency on the Financial World at Large

Even though Cryptocurrency is still in its infancy stage, its effect on the financial environment has already started showing. It's already causing growing curiosity and concern among conventional participants. Cryptocurrencies like Bitcoin, Litecoin, Ethereum and Ripple are starting to flex their muscles in the financial world so far as they have become popular currency alternatives for online transactions in many different industries. Users may avoid expensive foreign exchange services provided by banks and conventional payment processors by using cryptocurrencies for cross-border payments or money transfers. Besides that, cryptocurrencies are a better option since they replace banks as middlemen and are accessible; thanks to the public ledger makes them especially appealing to customers as an alternative financial system. In South Africa, for example, a whole host of companies, including tourism, retail and IT, accept Bitcoin as payment (eg Bidorbuy, Takealot and WeFix). Elon Musk's Telsa now exchange his cars for Cryptocurrencies.

Additionally, Cryptocurrencies are also increasingly used as investment instruments, but there are fears that this might be a bubble. As experts explained, "The current Bitcoin bubble is one of the most extreme examples ever witnessed in recent time. Over the past few decades, we've seen several bubbles (the global property bubble in the mid-'90s, the dotcom bubble, the silver bubble of 2001 etc.) While in nearly all these cases, asset prices increased by 1000% or more. The common trait was that the prices took at least a decade to inflate. In the bitcoin network, the price increased by more than 1000 per cent in just two years! " The Long Run Cryptocurrency, like any other emerging financial product or service, will face challenges in the future, particularly because it operates in an unregulated setting. Solving problems like fraud, network congestion, high fee costs, turnaround times, the risk of national government regulation and taxation, blockchain size, hyper-volatility, and ensuring high standards of safety and security will keep the crypto community busy for a long time. With that in mind, judging by the people's interest in the concept and its antecedent potentials, the Cryptocurrency looks set to have an impact on the financial landscape. To different people, Cryptocurrency will mean different things. Some people see it as an investment, while others see it as a risk, and still, others see it as a way to move money easily and safely around the world. Some investors are seeing Cryptocurrency as best suited as a means of long-term savings while some use it as cash for spending and making purchases.

Cryptocurrency Is For Saving.

It's simple to point to the long-term trend of major Cryptocurrencies steadily increasing in value over time and conclude that Cryptocurrency is a good investment. For instance, we can see a long-term growth trend in Bitcoin, which started at less than a penny per coin and is now worth over $50000 per coin. The same can be said for other major Cryptocurrencies, like Ethereum and Litecoin, for example.

This indicates that, amid periods of high uncertainty, crypto can be an excellent long-term investment vehicle for certain people.

You may be wondering why the cryptocurrency is such a successful long-term investment tool. To satisfy your curiosity, let's take a look at the US dollar. If you buried a

$100 bill for ten years and then dug it up and tried to spend it, the bill's buying power (or value) would be much lower than it was when you first buried it. Inflation is the explanation for this. In simple terms, national currencies are still losing value. This is a deliberate sharp decline that is often regulated or directly affected by central banks.

Let's say instead of burying a $100 bill, you buy $100 in Bitcoin, store it in a paper wallet, and bury it. When you come back to it 10 years later, your $100 worth of Bitcoin will almost certainly be worth a lot more than that when it was buried.

This is partly because Bitcoin is the polar opposite of inflationary properties. It is deflationary. That means it was designed to go up in value over time due to its limited supply. While governments can print money as much as they want, no one can create more Bitcoin than the network will allow through mining. Its supply is tightly regulated by the network and cannot be altered by anyone, including Satoshi Nakamoto, the inventor. This deflationary design feature is what makes Bitcoin and other Cryptocurrencies like it so appealing for long-term storage and savings. Bitcoin and other Cryptocurrencies were created to increase in value.

The Best Cryptocurrency for Spending

Can Cryptocurrency be used for spending and as cash now that we've discovered that it can be used to save money in the long run? Surprisingly, the answer is yes as well, but with certain qualifications. Cryptocurrencies have a level of independence, freedom, and versatility that has never been seen before. They have unrivalled comfort and virtually unlimited access to everyone and anything. At any time, any sum of money can be sent to everyone. There are no bankers, geographical limits, banking holidays, wire transfer cutoff times, or anything else along those lines. As a result, blockchain has the potential to be the ultimate national currency substitute. Bitcoin, for example, maybe the world's first truly international monetary type of currency. Because of its volatility, Cryptocurrency is equally suited for investing as it is for saving. In simple terms, volatility refers to the price or buying power of Cryptocurrency fluctuating continuously. Businesses will find it difficult to accept Cryptocurrency payments as a result of this. Many businesses likely fear that if they receive payment at 10 AM for a specific equivalent dollar amount, that value could drop by 5 PM and the company could potentially be facing a loss of revenue. Individuals will be concerned that the money they spent on Monday will be worth even more on Friday, resulting in them having effectively overpaid for whatever they purchased.

There are, however, a few possible alternatives. The use of a stable coin is one example. Stable coins are digital currencies that are intended to have a fixed value tied to something else, such as the US dollar. That means if you spend five units of a stable coin that's linked to the US dollar to buy a latte; those same five units will have the same relative value to the dollar six months later. This lack of volatility is very useful when it comes to using Cryptocurrency as cash. It's also likely that, when Cryptocurrencies evolve, their values will ultimately stabilize, just like financial markets do today. For example, major national currencies like the US dollar go up and down in value every few minutes much in the same way that bitcoin does. However, the amount by which the value changes is very minimal. Furthermore, since most major national currencies are stable, companies are comfortable offering their prices in a national currency that does not fluctuate minute by minute.

This implies that major Cryptocurrencies will mature to the point where businesses would feel confident listing prices for products at a fixed Cryptocurrency rate in the coming years. Since the exchange rate for Bitcoin has become much more stable, McDonald's may decide to build a new value menu in which everything costs 0.000001 BTC.

If you want to save money for the long run without having to depend on banks and their infamously low-interest rates, Cryptocurrency might be a good option. If you need to send money across borders regularly and don't want to pay high money order fees or be constrained by national boundaries, using Cryptocurrency as cash might be the way to go. Whatever your reaction, Cryptocurrency is likely to provide you with everything you need. It's also almost assured that Cryptocurrency would do much better than its conventional counterpart.

CHAPTER EIGHT
FOREX TRADING

Get the Right Knowledge about Forex

If you are new to investing and are looking forward to a medium to invest in, then you should consider exploring Forex trading. Forex is nothing but trading currency. This currency business is very stable compared to other trading business. Forex is very capable of making any investor wealthy in a very short period. Having said this, you must understand that there are some risks involved in Forex trading. These risks are common in any investments. So if you plan to invest in Forex trading then my advice would be to take some time to understand how the whole system works. Once you are familiar with the whole concept then you can start investing in currency trading.

With the unreliability of the stock market these days, more and more people are looking into Forex trading because it's easier to make money in Forex trading than in any other financial markets out there, and the risks involved are notably less compared to other investment options.

The most important thing in beginner investing for Forex trading is keeping yourself updated. Make it a point to read the newspaper every day. Don't just turn right away to the business section; the value of a particular currency rests on many factors, including politico-economic issues and natural disasters in the country of that currency. It's best if you read every page of the paper. Moreover, the market landscape of Forex trading changes every day, that's why you must make it second nature to keep yourself abreast of the changing market value of different currencies, especially the major ones, so you know what to buy and what to sell. Don't forget to take down notes. While it is exciting, Forex trading is in truth a hit and miss thing. There's no or little insider information and the values are constantly fluctuating, not fixed. Remember to keep a record of all your losses and your profits. This is the only way you can point out your mistake and avoid them in the future.

Why You Should Consider Investing In Forex

Despite several businesses that may attract you with bogus quick profits, why should you opt for investing in Forex? Here is a list of the reasons why you should consider Forex and it just might compel you to invest some money in Forex Trading.

1. Largest Financial Market

With $1.5 Trillion (yes, you read it right, it's $1.5 Trillion) being traded daily, Foreign Exchange (Forex) has become the largest financial market since the past 3 decades and its domination has only increased if anything. Forex Trading was left to the professionals till recently. However, now even average investors are willing to invest in it having witnessed its amazing capacity. This explains the sudden surge in the Forex market.

2. Leverage In Foreign Exchange Trading (Forex)

Frankly speaking, no business gives you leverage as that of Foreign Exchange or Forex (FX) for short. No hidden formulas, no confusing strategies or no professional knowledge required; all you need is a decent application of technical analysis along with a logical money strategy. Of course, leverage can be as harmful as beneficial. No hindrance on risk management means this high leverage can lead to potential high losses or high gains.

3. Trading 24 Hours On Forex

Forex is a 24 Hours trading opportunity. It's not going to be like you wait for the Forex shop to open. You will trade Forex 24 hours a day, from Sunday 5:00 p.m. to Friday 4:30 p.m. as a Forex Trader. This means you can do trading at your convenience and based on your schedule. It also provides you with the opportunity to act immediately upon golden breaking news from the market.

4. No Commission For Forex

There is no commission charged towards your profits on Forex. You are allowed to keep 100% of the profits that you make by trading on the Forex Market. Thus, this makes Forex Market an attractive and lucrative field of business especially to those who would deal regularly.

5. High Levels Of Liquidity Of Forex

Another crowd-puller is the high liquidity factor of Forex. Since seven major currency pairs account for nearly 90% of all currency transactions, these currencies have market stability, smooth patterns, and strong liquidity. The liquidity is mainly coming from the banks that offer cash flow to the average investors, organizations and market professionals.

6. Steady Trading Prospects

The Forex market is never stagnant; it's always on the move. Traders can most easily work in a growing or falling market because Forex trading requires buying and selling currencies.

This is due to the simple fact that there are always trading prospects whether a currency is rising or falling as it's co-related to other currencies.

Hence it does not matter whether the market is rising or falling, there are always opportunities for successful trading. All you need is to have a good trading strategy. With an amazing speed, even large transactions are conducted in a matter of seconds.

Along with these major advantages, there are other plusses like the large profits the Forex Trading promises. It is very much possible for an amateur investor to gain decent profits provided he has made a good study of the market before investing.

Why Forex Trading Is Better Than Stocks And Shares

Here are some of the reasons why investors find Forex investment quite stable compared to stocks and shares trading:

1. Studies have shown that even when the stock market went down throughout the world the Forex investors were still doing well. It has been proven that the currency market is more stable than the stock market and can handle the changes in the financial world more efficiently than any other trading business.

2. Unlike other trading businesses, to start investing in Forex you don't need to have huge capital. You can start by investing with a small capital and once you have consolidated your position then you can go in for big money. It has been proven that even with small investments anybody across the world is capable of making huge benefits for themselves.

3. Forex trading is fairly easy to understand and fairly easy to operate. Since the whole system is computerized you can set your limit of transaction and this can prevent you from losing any money. Now that we have established how

Forex investment is a better option than any other trading business out there we can focus our attention on some of the iron rules of Forex investment.

Basic Rules For Trading In Forex

• Rule 1

Do not invest everything and become bankrupt. This is perhaps the most important rule that one needs to follow. It is very vital that one should not get all too excited and invests all your savings into Forex trading. You need to invest only the money which you have in excess to currency trading.

• Rule 2

Do not be too hasty in making decisions. This rule applies to all investments. You must take your time to understand the ins and outs of currency trading. Only then can you make big decisions. Do not try to experiment without any knowledge about the system. This will only result in the loss of your money.

Virtually anyone can get lucky sometime or another and make a profit in the Forex market by trading only a few times because there are moments in which the exchange of currency pairs moves up or down and by following trends and entering in the right moment one could easily generate profits. Despite this, every investor in the Forex market should keep strictly his strategy to achieve better results in the long term investment abiding always to his predetermined risk appetite.

The following are the main points that allow traders to stick better to their strategies and achieve the right trading attitude.

1. Profit and Loss Possibilities

When you open a position, keep in mind the likely cost-benefit ratio. You should be sure that it is more likely to gain than lose in a specific transaction, so that after losses are deducted a positive number remains which is your profit. In other words, you should not open a position, if you do not have any reasons for doing so like an indication from economic or technical analysis. Besides, your earning potential should always be greater than the loss potential, preferably in a ratio of 1:2. In practice, this means that if you open a position, you should assume that you will earn

20 pips and if something goes wrong, you will lose only 10 pips. Forex trading platforms determine such limits by using the *stop-loss* (closing a position after a certain loss) and *take-profit* (closing a position at a predetermined profit).

2. Keep Your Emotions in Check

One of the most important and difficult aspects from all sides of investing in Forex trading is the ability to control your emotions. This means the ability to wait for a really good time to open a position, wherein the risk-return is high. Investors should approach the market without emotion, both during winning and losing transactions. After losing a trade, one should not allow his ego to persist by trying desperately to win back the lost trades. After reaching a certain profit, you should also remain calm and continue to stick to your strategy. Please note that the market did not change due to your transaction in any way, so neither should your strategy change.

3. Investing Can Also Mean Losses

If you decide to invest in the Forex market, you should think about great profits. But the fact is that every single investor goes through bad periods of losing trades that have no logical explanation whatsoever. Such a phenomenon, without proper money management, can lead to discouragement and in some cases zero deposit. This is especially true for beginners. Experienced traders are well aware that repeated consecutive losses are an integral part of any strategy in the Forex market. Of course, it is also crucial to have great management of your funds, have good risk management skills and be extremely resilient to stress.

CHAPTER NINE
TURN YOUR WEIGHTLIFTING HOBBY INTO ANOTHER PASSIVE INCOME SOURCE

Weightlifting is generally broken down into various categories - bodybuilding, powerlifting, Olympic weightlifting, and general health and fitness pursuits. And while each varies in philosophy and execution, weightlifters in general share one common trait - they love workouts and time spent in the gym.

In many cases, if not most, successful weightlifting also involves weightlifters getting enough sleep, maintaining a healthy diet, and using various vitamins and supplements to keep them healthy and maximize the results of their weightlifting.

Sound familiar?

So tell me, does it make sense to put in all that effort, to craft a healthy mind, body and lifestyle, just to spend 40 hours a week in a job you hate? Or even in a job that's OK, but still, brings stress into your life on a daily or weekly basis? We all know stress can be bad for the body and the mind, so why go through it to your detriment to make someone else wealthier? Sounds kind of counter-productive to all your healthy weightlifting lifestyle, doesn't it?

What if there was a viable alternative?

Fortunately, there is! If you've been weightlifting for a while successfully, you've no doubt noticed beneficial changes in your strength, energy, body shape and general attitude. And those around you, in the gym and out, have likely also been noticing and commenting. People are starting to ask how you lost weight, tightened up your midsection, built more muscle or have the time and energy to maintain your fit lifestyle, aren't they? And therein lies the answer to the work/lifestyle conundrum...

Huge numbers of people go to the gym on a daily basis but don't achieve the same effect as you. They may not have the knowledge of proper weightlifting procedures, they may not know which exercises are best to meet their goals, or they may not even have set specific goals yet, leaving them unable to gauge what works and what is wasting their time.

And for every one of them, there are 5 - 10 people outside the gym who want a healthy lifestyle, who want to lose weight, who want to be stronger or just generally want to improve their body before venturing out to the beach in their newest bikini or swim trunks. Many of them are intimidated by the idea of going to a gym and want to train at home, but they have no idea how to start. Others aren't intimidated, but they aren't overly motivated - yet.

Easy to see how YOUR weightlifting, diet and lifestyle knowledge and experience can help them, isn't it? Fortunately, you can start building your personal training business part-time, investing as much or as little time each week as you have available, at any point through the day or night that you choose to work on it. And unlike a lot of other home-based businesses, you have a great deal of control over how fast your business grows.

Start by doing some quick research online to see which certification best suits the style of weightlifting you want to coach. You might want to start with training to become a Certified Personal Trainer (CPT), a Certified Fitness Instructor (CFI) or even a nutrition coach. Over time you may want to get all three along with other, more specific certifications, but for now, choose the one that's most directly related to the type of weightlifting you love participating in. You're more like to stay motivated and complete the certification if you love the subject, and you'll also be learning new information to help your own weightlifting results.

While you're working toward your first certification, set up and start posting to your own health and fitness social media accounts. These will be your 'store-front windows' to the weightlifters and wannabes, so don't skimp - at a minimum set up profiles at Facebook, Instagram and

Twitter. If you're already a member or know of other social media sites you'd like to use, so much the better.

From this point on, make sure you're in compliance with any local laws and bylaws regarding home-based businesses and speak to your insurance professional as to whether you need liability insurance when dispensing exercise instruction, especially with the potential hazards for people new to weightlifting whether they are training at the gym or training at home.

While it's not necessary to have your weightlifting certifications to start training people, it certainly adds to your credibility when getting started, at least until you have some success stories from your initial weightlifting clients. But you can still do a lot to launch your business while you're still working toward those certifications.

Are you going to set up a private training area in your garage, basement or spare room? Or are you looking to train people virtually, providing them with the necessary guidance through video chats and pre-prepared workout routines tailored to their goals? Either way, let the word out that you're looking for a couple of weightlifting friends or acquaintances who are looking to get started or get better results, and that you're willing to train them for free or a reduced fee to be able to use them as examples of your training prowess.

And from there you're on your way to your own home-based business, turning your weightlifting hobby into your profession. As you garner more certifications, more clients, and a bigger social media following in the weightlifting and fitness industry, you'll find your knowledge, results, reputation and income can all increase regularly in line with the time and effort you invest in your new home-based business.

At some point, you'll be able to decide to keep it part-time or go full-time with your weightlifting coaching - and whether to continue to do it as a home-based business, set up your own personal training gym or make arrangements with a local gym to take your business there. In any event, you'll have the joy and satisfaction of knowing you turned your passion for weightlifting from your hobby into your profession, letting you operate on your own terms at your own schedule in a home-based business in a field you're already truly passionate about - weightlifting!

Video Assistant Expert

The voyage in becoming a virtual assistant is a joy ride. Everyone will undergo challenges in the first few steps especially if they are not computer savvy. For someone in this line of work, you must necessitates staying up with technology, because if you don't, you'll say things like "how are they doing it?" or "I think that's difficult," when the fact is that all we need to learn are a few basic acts to get together with the younger generation. So, let's begin with two simple items that we believe are unimportant but are essential for being a VA.

1. Facebook

What is your account title used on this site? Is it your real name or a different one that you just made up? Okay, let us begin with that when you're trying to look for a job, and you're using a different name that cannot be found easily on the internet then your client will think that it is a scam that you are not a real person. That's why you need to correct it and to indicate your first and last name and also be careful in all your posting because it will reflect your reputation. Most people today will upload everything on social media like when you're going to a party or drinking liquor, as much as possible avoid posting it because the client might think that you are an alcoholic and not capable of the job. So be careful with it.

2. Email

This kind of communication is a bit disregarded nowadays because of the availability of Messenger, Skype, Viber and many others but in the business world this conveyance is important. They used it to educate customers and clients about the firm's brand. That is how important it is to them, so how about your email is it still working or do you still remember the password? Let us talk about it, your email profile should look professional such as indicating your full name. You must also be familiar with how to use the "cc: CARBON COPY" or the "bcc: BLIND CARBON COPY" to keep all information secure.

We have known virtual assistant work is challenging especially for beginners. Being part of this industry today is a bit demanding, but it is a wonderful opportunity for everyone to have a career at home especially for the parents who still want to gain income without leaving the house and sacrificing family time. So here are some tasks you can start to apply for being a VA:

- **Email Manager:**

Most people communicate through email nowadays and that's why companies need people who will manage with their email account. Their job is to reply to the customer questions about the business product or services. Inbound email administrator will require a fast typing speed because this is a form of customer service.

- **Social Media Manager**

Everyone today is active in social networks such as Facebook, Instagram, Twitter, YouTube and many others. Here the firm wants someone to oversee their account regularly like posting and also might include replying some comments if needed.

- **Content Writer**

This is for people who love writing and have a very imaginative or creative work that the client needs. Being an author is good for those moms who are at home because they can write about their life being a working mom at their residence, about also their children especially they have a more imaginative mind, or you can compose any stories according to the requested topic by your client. Here you will draft stories for them.

- **Customer Service Representative**

This is for companies that are looking for an outsource agent who will answer incoming calls. Your job is to answer the calls and resolve the customer concern with the product or services that your client offer. Here you must have good communication skills, speak English, data entry because they will require you to document what happened in your call and have a broad understanding because sometimes they will talk about different things, but their complaint is a lot more different. There are criteria's that are required like a computer, head seat, internet speed and quiet working surroundings.

These are only for the beginners who don't have any skills or experience in graphic designing, appointment setting, hotel ticketing/booking, bookkeeping and many other jobs that are offered by a VA. Other aptitude/skills can be acquired by enrolling yourself in any VA classes that will help you to get or attract more clients because you offer many services, or if you are internet savvy, YOUTUBE is helpful for you. On that website, you can watch tutorials about many other skills that you can use as a VA. Nowadays expertise is more important than those courses that you finish because the ability is more helpful in looking for a job or career. Even though being a virtual assistant is quite tedious and also requires a lot of mastery but do the best you can and leave a good impression on your client this will build your reputation for a good start. So take a step, start to build your career being a Virtual Assistant today.

CONCLUSION

Staying at home and making all the money you need is a special kind of feeling you will cherish for life. The ability to build passive income is what allows you to quickly grow your wealth with relative ease. The freedom that comes with working from your home is out of this world. Although, it comes with its own relative and unavoidable challenges too. For instance, you will have to get a work office in your home where all your working equipment will be kept safe away from your kids and family members.

One thing is certain, you might not start making the big and fat income as a freelance worker in the beginning but with consistency and persistence, you get into the mix of things and start making the multiple-zero figures.

Another challenge you might face working from home will be people trying to short-pay you thinking your cost of doing business isn't much and such, you should charge less than another company offering the same services.

It should also be noteworthy to state that you don't start making millions immediately you start your online jobs working from home; it requires patience and hard work. It is also very easy to fall for scams online. You're probably dealing with a con if you see phrases like "big money for nothing" or "make money today." The reality is that if you want to make money online or offline, you must put in the effort. Better yet, stay away from those phony websites. You will see dozens of them when you search online. You will make money online when you can create the right websites for the right niches.

You must do away with the mentality of the employee. This will lead you to nothing in terms of money and business success. You need to look out for new ways to generate sales. You also need to be assertive and proactive. Online scams take advantage of employee mentalities many times to get your hard-earned money. Most of the business opportunities out there are scams. Please understand that you need to work if you want to make money online. I cannot stress this fact enough. Push-button income and traffic are for those with lots of experience and cash in the Internet marketing world.

It is also important to use the right delivery option for your product. These options might be mp3, eBook, and video and so on. You can send the product via email, instant download and so on. Sometimes you need to send a physical product to the buyer. Please make sure that your client will get the product. If you do not want to tarnish your reputation, you need to check the background of those with whom you plan to work. We cannot stress enough the importance of a thorough background check.

CPSIA information can be obtained
at www.ICGtesting.com
Printed in the USA
BVHW090547090621
609011BV00011B/2386